Bodies that Hum

poems by

Beth Gylys

*For Janelle
With all best wishes
for your writing &
with thanks.
BG*

*Allegheny College
2005*

Silverfish Review Press

Copyright © 1999 by Silverfish Review Press.

Published by Silverfish Review Press
P.O. Box 3541
Eugene, OR 97403

ISBN: 1-878851-12-8
First Edition.

This publication was funded in part by a publisher's fellowship from
Literary Arts, Inc. of Portland, Oregon.

Cover photo copyright © 1991 by Leeanne Schmidt.
Cover design by Valerie Brewster, Scribe Typography.
Text design by Rodger Moody.

Manufactured in the United States of America.

Acknowledgments

The author wishes to thank the editors of the publications where these poems originally appeared or are forthcoming.

Alabama Literary Review: "The One I Love"

Antioch Review: "Family Reunion—Aunt Vern's Two Cents"

Boston Review: "Do Not Dive Head-First," "Hard Luck," "My Savior in the Form of a Bus," "Personal," "Preference," "The Spectator"

Columbia: A Journal of Literature and Art: "How I Was"

Mudfish: "Easy Life"

The New Republic: "Success"

The Paris Review: "Marriage Song," "Not an Affair, a Sestina," "The Trouble With Love Poems about Men"

Ploughshares: "Pursuit of Happiness" and "Three Poems"

Poetry East: "Balloon Heart"

Poetry Northwest: "Split"

The Portland Review: "Afterwards" (under the title "After the Fact")

South Coast Poetry Journal: "Knots"

The Southern Review: "Photographer" and "Fat Chance" (under the title "Second Chance")

"Pursuit of Happiness" was also included in the *1996 Anthology of Best Magazine Verse*

Some of the poems in this collection appeared in chapbook form under the title *Balloon Heart*. Lexington: Wind Press. *Wind* magazine also reprinted "Balloon Heart," the title poem of the chapbook.

I am additionally grateful to David Lehman for choosing to feature my villanelles in the *Boston Review.* Also thanks to the University of Cincinnati Research Council, the Taft and Elliston Foundations and Bob and Charlotte Lanzit for financial support.

I am grateful to so many who assisted me with the writing and revision of this book. Thanks to Anne McCarty, Linda Buturian, Dina Ben-Lev, Dirk Stratton, Dave Smith, Denise Duhamel and the faculty and students at the University of Cincinnati, especially Don Bogen, Jim Cummins, John Drury, Andrew Hudgins and Erin McGraw. Thanks also to Rodger Moody for choosing the manuscript and for his astute critical insights and careful attention to the work.

Table of Contents

For my mother and father.

Part I.

FAT CHANCE

Every day another broken heart.
We try, but fail, to find our perfect match.
We'd never get involved if we were smart.

The woman thought she'd have a second start.
She'd loved a married man for years, a lech,
who didn't give a damn about her heart.

"I'm mad," she told her shrink, "I'd fall apart
without him in my life—I'm too attached.
I wouldn't be involved if I were smart."

Working in Maine, she met a man named Bart,
who called her "hon" and wore a diamond watch.
She told him all about her broken heart,

her father fix, her need to put the cart
before the horse. She warned, "I'm such a wretch.
You wouldn't get involved if you were smart."

Still, he proposed. They planned to wed in March.
He died before that, at a tennis match.
"Cracked and chronic" defines a broken heart.
We'd never get involved if we were smart.

DYNAMICS

He imagines her greeting him at the door in nothing
but silk stockings. She thinks they ought
to go out and look at the stars, drink a bottle
of French Bordeaux on the roof of his Honda.

When he wonders whether to stroke her breasts,
she has to water the dying plant and balance
her checkbook. She's tired, but he wants
to lie awake all night, her skin pulsing next to his.

He doesn't even know quite what that means,
but he read about it somewhere. When she puts on
her leather coat and smiles languorously, he would like
to take off the leather coat with his teeth

and have her lie stomach-down on the kitchen floor,
the leaves of the dying plant strewn about her like petals.
She's going to dinner with a friend;
he's sulking at home because he has ideas,

and she only has inclinations, which could possibly
come together on a train bound for Switzerland,
but they live in Ohio over the Souvlaki King restaurant.
He thinks they ought to marry, but he's afraid to ask.

She's decided he's a bore, that she'll break
up with him this winter, but it's fall,
and the leaves beneath her feet sound like they did
in third grade walking home with Marty Comini,

her crush the whole year, and she's making pesto
in his seven-month anniversary gift—a blender
bought at a garage sale. "You used to be inventive,"
she says. *You used to take your clothes off more*

slowly, he thinks. But instead of saying so, he touches
her sleeve and sidles out on the fire escape.
Sirens blare as he drinks a glass of juice, watches
the neighbor's terrier bark frantically through the window.

SUCCESS

Peter was desperate. He hadn't had sex
since the separation and every woman he knew looked
good to him: Louise, the animal activist; Martha,
the musicologist; Miriam, buxom and capable,
once named likeliest to have the biggest family.
Even Lavender, ugly, strange as she was talking
of alien abduction, tantric episodes with the gods,
seemed mysterious and compelling. But each
was married, or engaged, or gay. He jacked off
in his laundry, scanned the personals. He'd left his first wife,
a nervous woman who never stopped cleaning,
vacuumed the carpets constantly, yelled if his shoes
weren't off at the doorstep. "How do you expect me
to keep this place clean?" she'd ask sharply.
Then she'd weep. It made him crazy.
"I wanted a wife, a family," he told his buddy Nick,
"not the maid from hell." So he moved out,
found an apartment across town, stacked
dirty dishes everywhere for weeks at a time,
and felt happy, ecstatic really, for a while,
but now, thinking of his wife, her slender body leaning
into the closet to put away his coat, her face flushed
as she pushed the vacuum over clean carpet, made him
horny and forgiving. "Maybe I was insensitive," he thought.
He decided one night to dial the old number.
"Hello?" Her voice brought tears to his eyes.
"Honey, I want you back," he blurted, "I miss you."
"Come home." (That sweet sense of clarity.)
He couldn't say all he felt: "I'll be there
in twenty minutes…I, I love you." Toothbrush,
clean underwear, quick glance in the mirror.
At the house, he buried his face in her chest.
"I'm sorry, so sorry." They had sex all night long.
"What was I thinking to leave this good thing?"
he mused, lying beside his dozing wife. "How perfect
she is, how sweet. Maybe we'll have a child."

He drifted off, dreamed of getting promoted
at work, a big party with lots of presents,
people slapping him on the back, saying,
"Big guy, I always knew you could do it."

AFTERWARDS

Your desktop PC is well-equipped to handle
every disaster from spilled coffee to a power surge,
which is only one reason I don't understand
how you can just stand there,
puzzling at the toes of your Reeboks,
as if you might think of an apology for yourself
or your lack of courteous love-making practices,
such as kissing me on the neck,
for instance, or taking off your tube socks,
which, after all, usually have holes, and anyway,
you told me you didn't believe in all that shit
about mutuality or marriage, so at least you could stop
curling up your lip like a frazzled Doberman
and fuck like you want to fuck
or leave like you're never coming back.

GHOSTS AND ASPIRATIONS

His former lover liked to send a memo
each time her research team was sent abroad.
Today he'd gotten a note postmarked in Rome.
"The view's delightful, wine with every meal.
I feel as though I'm living in a dream.
Above's my number, why not give a ring?"

Her notes were chatty, terse; each had a ring
of false pretension. "Great!" he spat, the memo
glaring from his desk. "*She* lives a dream.
I work ten hours a day. *She* goes abroad.
I'm happy just to have a decent meal."
He mimicked in her voice, "I'm off to Rome.

It's better than the Astrodome, to Rome,
to Rome." He pranced and sang until the *brring*
behind him made him stop. He ate a meal,
potato chips and Coke, and typed a memo.
"Serves me right, sleeping with that broad,"
he grumbled, thought about his lifelong dream

to make a million on his thriller. "A dream,
perhaps," he'd told his wife. (His mind would roam
to yachts, a summer home and trips abroad.)
"Unlikely, yes, but not beyond the range
of possibility." He'd saved a memo
from an agent he'd met once at a meal:

"I'd love to see your finished book. E-mail
me at this address." He'd torn a ream
of prose to shreds the week before. The memo
blurred with dust. That agent lived in Rome
three months a year, his authors all a string
of big shots. "I'm going to spend six months abroad

when I complete this book," he claimed, but bored
by all he'd written since that fated meal,
he sat and wondered if he ought not ring
the woman up for old time's sake. *She'll dream
of me forever,* he thought and smiled, *in Rome
or Arkansas.* His fingers traced her memo.

He dreamed her body sleek from showering,
the two of them abroad in Nice or Rome,
some wine, a dim-lit meal... He balled the memo.

THREE POEMS

Narcissist #1
I'm so amazing I could lick myself.

Narcissist #2
Did you see how well I licked myself?

Narcissist #3
I was so upset. They barely noticed the way I licked myself.

THE TROUBLE WITH LOVE POEMS ABOUT MEN

They're not of curves and shadows made.
They don't wear skirts to swoop and tease
the eye, nor toss their hair, nor sway.
So arduous to package men to please:
a slant of hip, or buttocks tucked in faded
jeans—they lack aesthetic flair. A spray

of curls might fan their brows, or bellies bloom
above their belts. To paint men in the best
of light requires certain skill. The groom
looks better if he's built. He'll fill
his tux with sculpted flesh. His chest
will taper to the cummerbund. Still,

what work to capture men's appeal!
A rise between the legs will also shade
and shape their usual lines. Alas, revealed,
the bulge is but a stick. We live dismayed.
It's difficult to bring men warm regard.
We try. Their love is always hard.

THE LIE

We worked together selling ads
on the phone. I called a hundred

churches and businesses a day,
and he would walk to my desk,

stare, smile. "How's it going?"
he'd ask. Looking, he practically

licked me, and I let him, too
bored to say stop. Thirty-eight,

his face square, too big for his body,
he was awkward with beagle eyes.

I didn't want him but didn't say
get lost. Married, two children,

he craved magic, better choices. Lunch
break we'd drive to the country

with Beethoven, talk about travel,
painting, art, his two teenage boys,

how he and his wife hadn't touched
for a year. The music surrounded me—

like water, I floated. Did he
think I could save him

taking hold of my lifeless hand,
asking are you okay, and me

staring at the cornfields? What
was I doing? And he believing

I really cared for him—was torn
up about the marriage—

what was I thinking? Finally
I moved, stopped answering

his calls, but still I remember
his eyes pleading as if to say:

let me out, let me out, how even
in the end I lied and said I'd write.

THE ONE I LOVE

Is quieter than dust. I haven't
felt his nimble fingers,
bit him on the neck.
He doesn't enter the room,
babbling about the hole in his shoe,
the crazy driver, the kid
who wouldn't move out of the way.
He takes my hand like air;
he touches my stomach like air;
he whispers nothing in my ear
more delicate than a feather.
He hears me sigh
then is instantly behind me,
I'm here; don't worry.
He looks into my eyes—
all the way through—
and sees whatever hides there:
buildings falling down,
handguns, quicksand.
I love that, he says,
breeze brushing at my cheek.
He never flinches,
never retreats into himself,
puckering like a mushroom.
He likes me always:
as I soak in the bath,
or twitch before sleeping,
wraps me in his arms,
and it feels like summer.
He never breathes loudly in my ear,
never begs: "Please, don't leave me."
I love him as the daylight
holds my window,
the smell of bread
drifts down the placid street.
I tell you, I am lucky.
He lives entirely for me.
But me, I live for on one.

Part II.

DO NOT DIVE HEAD-FIRST

Do not dive head-first in that puddle of mud,
Most people know a puddle's not so deep;
Wade, wade slowly into the brackish crud.

Though mud is fine between the toes, the blood
Is best inside the body. I beg you keep
Your head. Don't dive into that puddle of mud.

Young children love a mess and if they should
Discover puddles in the mud, they'd leap
And not wade slowly in the brackish crud.

Dogs all clipped and groomed, who mostly would
Obey, keeping their tresses tidy, heap
Their bodies into any puddle of mud.

Cows are thinkers; in rain, they chew their cud,
Musing on this world, and seem to weep.
They wade slowly through the brackish crud.

And you, my friend, don't fret you're not a stud.
Looks, like puddles, only go so deep.
Do not dive head-first in that puddle of mud.
Wade, wade slowly into the brackish crud.

HARD LUCK

Allen Jones could not believe his luck.
He'd asked this woman Liza out for weeks.
All he really wanted was to fuck.

Now, first date, she sat there in his truck,
glancing in the mirror at her cheeks,
while he bought beer, amazed at his good luck.

About three miles away from home, a buck
jumped in the road. Allen slammed his brakes
and swore in silence, "Goddamn deer, you fuck

this night up, I swear I'll shoot you dead." The truck
began to spin. Allen woke to aches
all through his upper body. "What hard luck,"

he heard a strange voice say. Then someone stuck
him with a needle. He'd caused two other wrecks,
broken his jaw and ribs. He'd hoped to fuck;

instead, he lay in bed and had to suck
things through a straw for four depressing weeks.
He hadn't ever heard of such bad luck.
All he'd really wanted was to fuck.

SOME NIGHTS

Some nights the dark can press against the chin.
You see it all so clearly: life's a drag,
a game we're forced to play but never win.

One night Ed woke, forgetting where he'd been.
Dreams swam past him like a game of tag.
Alarmed, he pressed a pillow to his chin,

and felt the dark, which seemed to lurch and spin,
consume his self (or was his self the bag—
and night his soul—a force he couldn't win?).

He finally stood and searched the house for gin,
but only found scotch tape, a dirty rag.
He sat and put a fist up to his chin

and everything grew far away and thin,
the world a kind of drooping, soggy flag,
symbolic of the game he'd never win.

Perhaps we'll know the truth before we're gone.
That night Ed felt he dangled from a crag—
the dark pressed down so heavy on his chin—
as if to force the point: he couldn't win.

...iE ADJUNCT

He takes the bus to teach another class.
He's tired. He's hungry for a steak and fries.
He puts in extra hours. He busts his ass

to pay the rent, feed the dog, amass
a horde of bills. No matter how he tries—
he'll ride the bus a thousand times to class—

and still he's never out of debt. He has
the Ph.D., a book that he'd revise
if only he had time. He busts his ass.

He's still committed to the work he does.
He'll grade his tests till dawn, realize
it's time to shower and catch the bus to class

where Jerry's late, Jane offers tongue to pass.
Jill's homework isn't done because, she sighs,
"My mom's been ill for days." "Your mother's ass,"

he thinks, but only nods. "I'll never last
until I'm really hired." He shuts his eyes
and takes the bus to teach another class.
He puts in extra hours. He busts his ass.

FALL

The leaves are turning, and it makes him itch
to change his name, hitchhike to Vermont.
Ted wonders if it's like that with the rich.

Lounging by the pool deciding which:
to sail the yacht, or dress up for the hunt?
He'd see the leaves were turning, have an itch

for poverty: "Forget the sushi, a sandwich—
chipped ham on Wonder Bread—that's what I want."
"Perhaps," he thinks, "it's like that for the rich."

"Do they tire of limousines, or bitch
they never rode a Greyhound bus to Flint?"
The leaves are falling; he wonders, "Do they itch

for simpler lives: a trailer with a hitch,
their friends in housecoats drinking Bud out front."
He often thinks he'd like to be so rich

that he could spend his time acquiring kitsch,
and wealth would seem a burden to lament.
The leaves are dying, and it makes him itch.
He wonders if it's like that for the rich.

THE SPECTATOR

He loved to look at bodies, so he said.
His high-rise faced another just as tall.
He didn't care for women in his bed,

preferred them through the window. He wouldn't wed,
he vowed. "Why bother? From here, I see it all."
"I only like to look," he often said.

"A neighbor pulls a dress over her head,
and I'm a happy man. Marriage is hell.
I don't need a woman in my bed."

His favorite window overlooked a spread
of neon signs. He called the woman "Nell,"
who often stood there looking out, he said,

half-nude. And while he watched she'd sometimes shed
her clothes right there. "I think she isn't well,"
he told me once. "I watch her from my bed.

She's lovely, but she seems distracted, sad."
If he was ever lonely, who could tell?
He loved to look at bodies, as he said.
He didn't want a woman in his bed.

MARRIAGE SONG

Some have affairs. They never stop to think
until they're begging for a second chance.
(We love and learn we sometimes need a drink.)

Impatient with his life, he quipped, "We blink,
we're forty: with wives, kids, retirement plans."
Some have affairs. It isn't what they think.

He saw this woman at the skating rink,
watching their sons play hockey from the stands.
He fought the urge to ask her for a drink.

She wore those stretchy pants, a long faux mink,
slid next to him and said, "Hi, my name's Nance."
He wanted her right there. He couldn't think.

They fucked in hotel rooms, designer pink,
drank cheap champagne. He signed her underpants.
They fucked and ordered something else to drink.

His wife broke all the dishes in the sink,
took both the kids and flew first-class to France.
Some have affairs—it's never what they think.
We sigh and shake our heads. We have a drink.

Part III.

BALLOON HEART

For days after the wedding,
she left the balloon heart
hanging on her car's antenna.
She liked the way the limp
bubble drooped and bounced
each day becoming emptier,
heavier, less like a celebration.
After three weeks it snowed.
By then the heart had slid down
until it touched the hood,
and as she drove, the thing,
now frozen, knocked and knocked
like knuckles on a hard wood desk,
like an ice pick chipping away.

KNOTS

What I liked most was when I'd say I had to go
and he'd brush my hair sometimes fifteen minutes.
I'd stand watching in the mirror
while he pulled it all back
over my shoulders and untangled the knots.

He was a short man, his head a bit too large.
His hair curly, he played guitar for me,
sitting on a tall, wooden barstool.
He played folk songs, love songs,
with his face scrunched and strained,
as if he was squatting on the toilet.

It would have been comical, except
for his wanting, those aching notes
he sang out of the squashed, tightened,
too-large head, eyes closed,
pouring himself into it.

He'd talk to me for hours on the phone
about his dreams, his plans
for the future—how he admired me.
And I listened with concern and confusion,
not caring for him, not enough.

But I was lonely and drifting.
To be honest I liked the attention.
I felt a fondness, a sisterly compassion.
I did nothing intentional to hurt him.
I just didn't say anything,
let him praise me, touch me.

We'd reach that point in the night
when he'd sit beside me, all pang,
all longing, bend over, and I'd think,
I wish he was still singing,
or already brushing my hair,
not hungry, pressing his lips, his curls
down to me like an animal thirsty for water—
his fingers waking my body,
and my body responding, deceiving.

What did I give him: an ear,
a soft morsel to stroke? Not filling
those holes, that need. My God,
his eyes like mouths.
I'd try and forget, lost in the motion
like seaweed caught in the tide.

If only it had been just hands! (He tender,
mournful, my guilt big as the bed, the room.)
Until I could say, "I really have to go."
We'd dress in the dimness, our backs turned.
And then, finally, he'd brush out my hair.

I could have stood for hours
feeling the tug and pull, as if the brush
untangled more: confusion released
or complications straightened after loving,
after not loving. My memories are all snarls.

WHY I LIKE TO LIE AWHILE LONGER

Because your face, your eyes, the whole of you
is with me, gently, a softening light
across a spray of petals. I'm of pastel colors
made, laced throughout the April garden.
Your hands against my skin, you touch the hearts
of delicate flowers. Our bodies breathing warm
against each other, mostly we don't move,
but lie, our limbs entangled, as if we were
two separate vines all twisted in one braid
until the eye becomes confused which loop
belongs to one, which to the other; I know
the sense of blending's false—we break
so easily apart—but still, I love you
soft inside me and us not quite alone.

THROUGH THE GLASS

As usual, you're in your office on the phone.
But when you see me coming, you shut your door
so I can't hear. Your latest news: another
wants you; you say that it's complex. You want
to keep things sane, to stay alone, married.
You're worried you might hurt us all. Of course.

You didn't have to tell me. I've felt you pulling
away as if we were attached. I watch you
through the glass; you're flushed, nervous with me
waiting here, though you talk as if I weren't
sitting at your door, my hands numb,
shaking with pain. How can we stop ourselves

from wanting? Do I touch you with my eyes?
You have a wife, me, and now this third;
we rotate around you like three human moons.
You turn; your hand is raised. What should I think?
What should I feel? I'd like to say it doesn't
matter. Should I lie to spare myself?

You act surprised when you come out: "Are you
okay? What's wrong?" as if it's nothing, nothing:
Why am I upset? You aren't so honest
after all, and I a moon whose face
is bruised with shade. I'll shine my harvest smile:
I'm fine, complicit in my sorry way.

Having felt your hands on fire with years
of longing, having felt my own hot fire
emerge to meet you, finally, finally, I'm bound
to you—we all are—held in our own ways.
You will love your women as you like,
and I will eat myself like homemade bread.

EASY LIFE

Doughnuts half-eaten on plates.
An answering machine
that can bake a loaf of bread.
Naked, we run to the bedroom.

In circles your hand smoothes my back.
How cold it is outside. Sometimes
a branch scrapes the window
like the nails of someone desperate.
I imagine he wears a worn tweed coat,
that his face is crazy, twisted.

*

You leave messages for me, saying:
sandwich, fart, garbage, spaghetti,
sex. Each word sounds the same.
I'm forgetting the meanings of things.
Through the window, I watch two women
fight over bottles in the trash.
I think of their hands
smelling of dead things;
I read "Dear Abby."

*

Have you noticed
how each hour sags
into the next? On weekends
our neighbor teaches manners
to his kids; we watch him press
their faces into dirt
till they yell: thank you,
please, please, you're welcome.

BRIEFLY

I suppose I shall love you
though I am scrubbing out the sink,
walking half-dulled to the drug store.
I suppose we will go on as we must,
forces moving us forward:
business arrangements, dinner,
conversations about the news.

Yet I'm weak for the slips of remembrance,
a certain phrase turning into you,
confusions of inflection,
or hands held up a particular way,
a laugh maybe, like glasses on a shelf
suddenly found by the sun—
you again—brilliant for a moment—
me too, yes, all at once and then not.

HOW I WAS

A day last spring. My hands smelled of carrots.
I don't know where it was I walked or stood—
a hill perhaps, a park. The sky was full

of mood the way it changed—the blue of it,
the blue but also the gray—that mixed and blurred
as light in dreams, as crowds. And I was right then

there, right there, between the carrots and
the pungent smell of green, the trees blown sideways,
their branches twisting, mixing, coming free. It wasn't

truth, but the sky, the wind, the clouds (and they
were not like continents or sheep, but simply white
wisps tumbling past). Imagine having stood,

your hand holding a streetcar rail, your hair
awash with wind, having heard the clanging bells
and felt the engine churning at your feet.

It's *that* I mean—the way it moves and moves
at times—your heart and something else. I wanted
nothing, and was nothing, and was fine.

LONG DISTANCE

Star, just inches from a slit of moon,
I think it's half a face drawn by a child.
I won't tell you that I saw this, this
so far from what I've come to understand
of smiles worn too long or the heavy weight
of eyes against my eyes. Tonight,
driving alone across too common country,
a blur of landscape, bulge of a tree, I feel
something more than what I'd say. Silence.
The dashboard glows with nothing like a promise.

I've come to see my life is not a prayer
but one mistake framed against another.
At home, I'll lift my eyebrows, softly say,
"It's good to see you," instead of, "It's over,"
leaving the door half-open as I turn.
But I still keep coming home again
(home, if home is where we are), my face
dark against the mirror of the windshield,
as I drive once more across the widening distance.

SPLIT

Everyone I know is crying
or should be crying.
I say their names each night.
Why do I do this?
The wind won't listen.
Neither will those two dark birds
that slip across the sky.
It's winter. Naked branches
aren't full of ache;
they neither hover, nor point,
nor feign like open arms.
They are simply growing,
flecked with knots and ridges,
etched by different shades of line.
Don't let me tell you how it is.
Go out. Look.
Life makes itself without us,
and a boy bounces
his bright red ball
along the sidewalk.
Not quite one of us.

PHOTOGRAPHER

Framing, you crouched, focused, captured, shot,
I watched you where I stood, your movements slow,
measured. Sparring with the light, you hoped
to hold the thing, to catch the proper angle,
came back along the path where arches rose
and sunlight burned my face. We walked a while,
then stopped again for ten or fifteen minutes.
Patient, I'd learned it takes a lot of time,
confining bits of world within a square.

At home, we relived Arches by the window,
holding each slide up to see the image.
"Look," we said, "this one's really good,"
and passed them back and forth across the table,
the cat meowing at our feet, and you,
annoyed. "Shut up!" you yelled, and grabbed for her.
I loved the colors of those slides, the orange-
pink of rock, rising from the sand,
the one of us standing by a bush,
your arm around my waist, your silly grin.

In albums of our many trips and visits,
there's more of me than you. Waist-deep in leaves,
I wave, or showing off my strength, I hold
your friend piggyback on the lawn—I'm bent,
laughing, his elbow hooked around my neck.
At Crater Lake, I stand in shorts and seem
exhausted, my hair flying loose, my eyes
squinting at such rich shades of blue.
That was before I flipped the car. You took that
too, the metal crushed like foil or paper
while I lay miles away in ICU.

In most, I seem content, holding the cat
or drinking coffee with my high-school pal.
What did I know or did I lose from then
to now? Here's one in Maine, the two of us
on bicycles—Acadia park—the ocean
beating the shore beneath the road we ride.

Is that the way we lose ourselves in time:
a wind or ocean chips away the land;
we wake one day to find ourselves surrounded,
water to our hips, the island gone?

Last year my parents came to see the house.
You and Mom installed an extra phone line
to run the modem that you'd bought. "You two
can talk through e-mail," said my mom. Her smile
stung; she never read me very well:
our own strained smiles still trying to believe
in what we were, still trying to deceive.
There are no pictures of that visit; you hardly
took the camera out all year. We never

did get copies of the wedding proofs.
The photos with the shadows that you hate,
and hardly any of our guests. We shrugged
and said, "What can we do? He is our friend—
he took them all for free." We rolled with things.
That was our way. When Sara came, the time
her husband threatened to find a whore, we made
the extra bed, drank tea and talked till late.
And when my cousin told us he was gay,
we gave him hugs, played Scrabble all night long.

The pictures end in New Orleans. Your friend
got married there last June; there's only one
of us together, riding the train, your hand
holding the rail above my head. We smile,
of course. We had to smile—this was a picture!
And then blank pages after that. I turn
and turn as if to find a future there—
us headed West, or fixing up the house—
as if the slots of plastic might be filled
with answers to the questions: what went wrong,
why love leaves us, or how to carry on.

SONG OF AN X

Don't think of me
as you pull
shirts out of the washer,
or wipe the chocolate
from your child's face.
Don't think of me
bathing, or slipping
from my dress.
Don't imagine my bare shoulders,
my hair hanging loose
as I dance through empty rooms.
Don't stop to think of me
as you take the hand
of your wife across the table.
Don't think of my thoughts,
my laughter, my umbrella,
my tongue, my tall black boots,
my way of sighing.
Don't think of me lonely,
or making love,
or lit darkly by candles,
as you step outside
to retrieve the morning paper,
dressed only in your bathrobe
and a pair of old gray socks.
Don't think of me.

Part IV.

THE ERRATIC GARDENER

She will not plant her love in rocky ground,
but longs to feel its bloom so much it hurts.
She tries to tend to every man she's found—

uncertain who she wants to take her hand.
Her married friends detest the way she flirts.
She will not plant her love in rocky ground,

but envies every couple she's around.
She watches men—the way they move, their shirts.
There's something good in every one she's found.

Her mother thinks she needs a wedding band,
presents the girl to all the men she meets.
She's liked a few, but still she stands her ground.

There's always one or two young men around.
She prattles on the phone in endless chats.
She gently teases every man she's found,

and drives each one she's with out of his mind.
She's coy then wholly his in fits and starts.
She will not plant her love in rocky ground,
so tries to tend to every man she's found.

PREFERENCE

Some people need a harsher kind of love.
I like the smooth soft wetness of our sex.
I like the gentle easy way we move,

our bodies blending in a fleshy weave,
our lips, torsos, tongues a sensuous mix.
Some people need a harsher kind of love.

One plays the master, the other plays the slave.
They plunge each other's depths with plastic dicks.
I like him gentle. I like his easy move

against me, desire rising like a wave
that draws us slowly to its crest then breaks.
Some women need a harsher kind of love.

A brutish forceful man is what they crave.
They scream and bite; they claw their lovers' backs.
I like the gentle, easy way you move,

and taste and touch my skin, without a glove,
or ropes to bind me. How could I relax,
confronted with a harsher kind of love?
I'll take the gentle, easy way we move.

MY SAVIOR IN THE FORM OF A BUS

"Do you believe in Jesus Christ our Lord?"
An old, balding man was in my face.
He wasn't someone who could be ignored.

I thought he'd go away if I looked bored.
I rolled my eyes and yawned. He kept his place.
"Do you believe in Jesus Christ our Lord?"

"I'm Jewish, give it up," I moved toward
the street, but then my heel caught on some ice.
I fell. "You see, He mustn't be ignored."

This guy, I thought, is someone for the ward.
But I was at his feet. "It must be grace,"
he said, held out his hand. "You know the Lord,

can work in wondrous ways." He'd struck a chord:
my days in Catholic school, a veil of lace,
the words a priest once said, that I'd ignored:

He'll come to you, carrying a sword.
And, Beth, how will you meet him face to face?
My bus pulled up just then, thank the Lord,
rescuing me from questions I'd ignored.

THE PLODDER

I jog to eat and take my jogging slow.
I wouldn't claim the effort makes me wise.
So much about this world I'll never know.

When other runners pass, I let them go.
For back street running, no one wins a prize.
I jog to eat and take my jogging slow.

Old Edy and her spaniel, Little Joe;
our paperboy; the men in suits and ties.
The stuff of early morning—this I know.

Emerging neighbors hail me as I go.
We do a dance acquaintanceships devise.
I smile or give a wave, but never slow.

The morning light can have a tranquil glow.
Alone I hum, trot over dip and rise.
The more I run, the less I need to know.

I focus on my breath—its ebb and flow—
and hope this helps delay my sure demise.
I jog to eat and take my jogging slow.
So much about this world I'll never know.

DESIRE

Your penis fits quite fine between my thighs.
Come lie with me a while, this life is hell.
We're nothing but our bodies. Close your eyes

and let me touch you. I could see it rise
when I walked in. I'm not ashamed at all,
your penis fits so well between my thighs.

Why must we talk? I hate how words disguise.
I love the way we touch, and taste and smell,
reacting with our bodies. Close your eyes

and feel the truth of sex. It signifies
our wish to find the other side, a spell
the penis weaves between another's thighs,

the taste we have to beat the thing that dies
and bind the other to the self. We'll still
be bodies: naked limbs and hungry eyes.

We might desire the things that money buys,
but more we want to feel our soft hearts swell,
to take the penis warm between our thighs,
feel nothing but our bodies, close our eyes.

PERSONAL

I want a man whose body makes mine hum,
who when he looks my way the sky goes hazy.
Don't call me if you're boring, crude or dumb.

Discussions about sports teams turn me numb,
and men who can't stop talking drive me crazy.
I want a man whose body makes mine hum,

who sweetly cries my name out as we come,
a sensual man, whose touch makes me feel dizzy.
Don't call me if you're angry, cheap or dumb.

I like full lips, bare skin, long winter nights, some
good red wine. I like to spend a lazy
morning with a man who makes me hum.

I like to wade in fountains just for fun,
to decorate my hairband with a daisy,
skinny-dipping, hopscotch, playing dumb.

I love good jazz, dancing till I'm numb,
deep snow, strong wind, a girl dressed up in paisley.
I want a man whose body makes mine hum.
Don't call me if you're rigid, mean or dumb.

Part V.

PURSUIT OF HAPPINESS

after Carlos Drummond de Andrade

Ned loved Betsy, a blond waitress who lived in the suburbs.
Only Betsy was in love with Peter, the race car mechanic,
who had muscles and a black Corvette, and wore a cross
inside his T-shirt. But Peter was half-crazy over Anne, his beautiful ex-
lover, who said, "You're nothing but a loser,"
left him to marry Chet, the insurance salesman, who was boring in bed
but who was climbing hand over hand up the corporate ladder.
At the dress rehearsal, Chet's sister Jane met Betsy,
and her heart had leapt with the force of a gazelle.
It was hopeless of course. Betsy couldn't stop talking about Peter:
his opalescent eyes, his enormous biceps. After months of despair,
Jane tried to hang herself, awoke in the Community Hospital
in the same room with Margaret, a nun from Minnesota
admitted for irritable bowels, who reminded Jane
of her sixth-grade teacher, also a nun, who'd kissed
her ear one day after school. Jane had a religious conversion
right there in the hospital, left her job as secretary at Finch,
Legatt, and White Legal Services, and joined the order—
Sisters of St. John of the Cross. Margaret, the nun, passed
away from complications. Betsy met a cross-dresser and
ran off with him to Venezuela. Peter enrolled at the local college to study
medical terminology. Anne had four children and gained 30 pounds.
Ned remained at home caring for his aging father,
a retired dentist, who ate spoonfuls of blender food till he died.

NOT AN AFFAIR, A SESTINA

You're crazy if you called this an affair.
We slept together, and I made you come.
No big deal. You've got a lot of strange
ideas. You think you know so much about me,
think because you've seen me naked that counts
for something. Just because I put my head

between your legs, because you gave me head,
you tell the world we've had some big affair.
We've been together twice—no one counts
that time behind my desk. I didn't come.
(How could I relax, you simply grabbed me?)
I'm not the one you need. You're really strange.

You try to make this seem important, this strange
relationship we have. I'm no head
to place upon a platter. I'm married. Me,
I'm not the kind of man who has affairs.
I like you—that is all. It doesn't come
to any more than that. Do you know what counts

in things like ours? I'll tell you what counts.
Let me put it simply: it's not that strange
to meet in places in the dark, to come
between your hopes and what you have, and head
for someplace warm and soft. To have affairs—
a real affair—is wrong. It seems to me

you give too much away. You're telling me
as well as all your friends these wild accounts
of us and me and our intense affair,
as if to have a little sex was strange.
I know you think I'm messing with your head,
but you're the one who kept this going. You came

to see me. You knew my life was set. I've come
to take things as they are: I know you want me.
It's hard to be alone, to move ahead
with no one there, when nothing seems to count.
Believe me, I've felt like that. You aren't so strange,
Listen, I do care; this wasn't an affair.

I hope you come to see that, take what counts
from what you tell me is a big affair,
and head to love more real than strange.

MY FATHER'S NIGHTMARE

His daughter's a poet. (Lord save us!)
And he's sitting at some big reading event,
held in some big city. She's reciting
a long narrative poem about an abortion,
and she keeps saying the word fuck.
Fuck, in fact, seems to occur three or four times
in every sentence she reads.
He can't stand the thought of her doing that.
Why does she need to say it in front of everyone?
He happens to be the honored guest.
She keeps telling jokes about him.
She talks about his martinis,
and how he always falls asleep on the sofa,
newspaper covering his chest.
He smiles wanly. She reads another fuck poem.
She reads a poem about kissing a woman.
It's clear she must have done this.
She describes the tenderness of lips,
the special hue of skin, the curves
and the moistness all so vividly.
He wonders, *Why can't she write poems about nature,*
something along the lines of Robert Frost?
He can't believe that's his daughter.
She winks at him. She asks him up on stage,
but he refuses. Now she gyrates her hips,
moving, he notes grimly, like a dog.
Why didn't she become a lawyer like her brother?
Or even a waitress—they make decent money.
He thinks, *Maybe I should go to the bathroom*
and sneak out the back door,
wonders, *Why did I fund all those years*
of college English? He's reading his menu,
holding it up, so it blocks out her face.
She recites a poem about a married lover.
He thinks he's going to puke.
She says the word fuck twice really loud,
and he's had enough. He gets up, turns,

knocks into someone's arm,
but it's only my mother shaking him awake.
"Honey, are you coming to bed?"
kitchen light behind her like a halo.
Life couldn't be better really,
house by the shore, endless martinis,
children gainfully employed.
Sure, his daughter's a little strange,
with her poetry, her divorce,
but she works hard, never asks
to borrow money. *She seems*
all right, he tells himself,
as he climbs the stairs to go to sleep.
She's always been a pretty good girl.

STUFFED

Years ago, you came home with a gift,
a white stuffed cat, all polyester fur,
a crown of it around her face, a sea
obscuring her oval body, little bow

nestled in a tuft above her head.
I combed her with a small pink plastic comb,
and hugged and held her. When I was five or six,
you coaxed me to the water at the shore

and lifted me above the waves when I
would start to scream. As we grew old, your laughter
cheered our dinners after two Manhattans
calmed your nerves. What presents did you covet

sitting at your house on that old porch-swing,
the house you lived in all your life, which always
smelled to me like dust, even though
your mother cleaned the place until her hands

were raw? Your mother, tiny, but strong as rock,
who wouldn't use the washing machine you bought,
but scrubbed clothes on the washboard till she didn't
have the mind to clean at all. What memories

haunt your evenings nights before you nap,
the paper open on your chest, the glass
beside you resting on a coaster, empty
but for melting ice? For you are fine

and doing well each time we speak and have been
all these years, although you've seen your father,
mother, younger brother buried. How
can you be fine? Our setter tore that white cat

into shreds when I was seventeen.
Poor dog, I yelled and smacked her till I cried.
You knew me when you brought that kitty home:
I was timid, quiet, shy at eight,

and loved small furry things. Now I'm
divorced and sad, but fine too, to you
and Mom. Eight hundred miles away, you call
on Sundays just to say hello. You traveled

to Chicago, Pittsburgh, Houston maybe.
That is what you do. You and Mom
become a chorus on the speakerphone.
She says, "Well that's all I have, Carl, how

about you?" "That's it for me." I don't protest.
We tally up our lives, the cities where
we've flown, the meals we've had. It's easiest
to love this way—I learned that best from you.

Hanging up the phone, I watch my cats.
Cleo's distant; she eyes me from across
the room. Alexis jumps up on my lap;
stretching her legs, she purrs so hard she shakes.

FAMILY REUNION—AUNT VERN'S TWO CENTS

"So, Dear, your mother says you got a divorce.
How could this happen? You seemed so much in love
when you got married. I saw you walking down
that aisle—you were floating. Anyway,
I said to your mother: I hope she's dating.
A shame to be alone—a girl your age—

so pretty too. When I was your age,
I had two babies, no time to think of divorce.
It wouldn't matter today. When I was dating,
things were different. We still believed in love
for life. Together, couples found a way.
I tell my kids they better not head down

that aisle until they're sure. My oldest, down
in Texas, his girlfriend's nearly half his age.
I've prayed that they'll break up, but now the way
it's going I'm sure they'll marry. 'Headed for divorce,'
I tell my husband. 'But, Verna, they're in love,'
he says. (He's such a romantic.) They're only dating

now, thank God. Of course, even dating
is scary these days, with AIDS, date rape. Just down
our street a woman's son got AIDS. You love
your kids as best you can, but…I've seen her age
ten years since he moved home. His whole divorce
was bad enough, but carrying on that way

and then to get so sick. Things aren't the way
they used to be. I'm probably dating
myself to say so, but I can't believe divorce
is any answer. It comes right down
to making a commitment. Kids your age
you think it's easy. You marry out of love,

and when that first glow fades, believe the love
is gone. There's got to be a better way
to make things work. You think a marriage
is fun and games—you want it just like dating.
In forty years, we've had our ups and downs,
but I never once considered divorce.

Down the road you'll see: love isn't dating.
There's a rhythm to the way a marriage
works. Divorce destroys the best of love."

FERVOR

In Central Park, a flasher blows a whistle,
whips out his cock
from beneath a tawny trench coat.
Meanwhile, two blocks down
where a hill banks beneath the shade of trees,
an eighteen-year old
reads his book and rubs himself;
a businesswoman on her way home from work,
turns onto the grass, kicks off her shoes,
recalls the time she came in the empty classroom,
her professor standing behind her,
his hands probing in her stockings,
"Oh, yes," he said. "Oh, baby."
And somewhere across town
a woman's back is thrust against the wall,
her legs around his waist,
"Oh yes!" she cries. "Don't stop!"
And then everyone is sensing it,
"Oh yes," they think,
and feel a stirring in their thighs.
Couples come together without meaning to.
Clothes fall to the floor,
and legs open spontaneously;
fingers curl, clutching air or bits of clothing.
Like the bodies of newborn babies,
bodies writhe and sing in monosyllables:
"Please," and "Oh, God."
And the noise becomes a chorus.
And the firemen glance up from spraying their hoses;
the women at the bakery go slightly rosy;
and the men on the subway
loosen their ties and look to their feet,
want to give themselves over
and let it squeal into the universe—
blind pigs, discontented cows,
full-throated, desperate, raw.

NO SIMPLE WISH

How long could I take to put on my coat?
How long could my hand linger on your doorknob?
I'd want to tell you something: "It's important
to count buttons," or "Remember
that funny kid with the huge feet," but
your face would go blank. I'm holding out my hand,
but you aren't here. You're sleeping,
or watching television, or out trimming
the forsythia. Evenings, the sky turns
orange and sirens rattle the streetlights
as I walk to the grocer's, or put away the linens.
How easy it is to be lonely in the dark.
You'll rest your head on the back of the big
armchair, let the spaces fill you,
the way water fills a garden pitcher.
I'll stand at my sink and wash out
the coffee pot, thinking, "My hands are red
but not like Valentines." Still,
I'll wish for a quiet rain streaming
down my windows, and the kiss,
the one that says, *I'm here, I'm here.*